Reposition
Yourself
Reflections

ALSO BY T.D. JAKES

Reposition Yourself

Not Easily Broken

Can You Stand to Be Blessed?

Ten Commandments of Working in a Hostile Environment

He-Motions

Cover Girls

Follow the Star

God's Leading Lady

The Great Investment

The Lady, Her Lover, and Her Lord

Maximize the Moment

His Lady

So You Call Yourself a Man?

Woman, Thou Art Loosed!

Mama Made the Difference

Reposition
Yourself
Reflections

*Living a Life
Without Limits*

T.D. Jakes

ATRIA BOOKS

New York   London   Toronto   Sydney

ATRIA BOOKS

A Division of Simon & Schuster, Inc.

1230 Avenue of the Americas

New York, NY 10020

First Atria Books hardcover edition November 2007

ATRIA BOOKS and colophon are trademarks of Simon & Schuster, Inc.

For information about special discounts for bulk purchases, please contact Simon & Schuster Special Sales at 1-800-456-6798 or business@simonandschuster.com.

Designed by Nancy Singer

Manufactured in the United States of America

10   9   8   7   6   5   4   3   2   1

ISBN-13: 978-1-4165-4758-7
ISBN-10:   1-4165-4758-4

If you just make minor adjustments and do a little bit of repositioning, you can live your life without any limits at all.

—*T.D. Jakes*

They that wait upon the Lord shall renew their strength. They shall mount up on wings like eagles. —They shall run and not be weary. They shall walk and not faint.

—*Isaiah 40:31 (KJV)*

Read This Before Repositioning Yourself

A little boy wanted to see an eagle fly. He put some sandwiches in his backpack, got his binoculars, and set out on the plains, saying, "I'm going out there to see the eagles fly!"

The sky was vast and seemed to stretch out forever like an endless blue blanket, but no birds were anywhere in flight. Then, in the distance, he spotted wings. Nooo. What he saw was a hawk. After a long wait, another bird came into view, and he grabbed his binoculars, only to discover—a big disappointment—it was a pigeon. He was about to head home, dejected, when far, far above his head he spied it. Yes! Aaaaahh—that's an eagle!

As the magnificent creature soared into the boy's view, he was awestruck. The boy had learned about eagles in school, but nothing had prepared him for this sighting of a real eagle.

When the eagle spreads his wings, from tip to tip he is

eight to nine feet long. The eagle can see two to three miles away. His vision is that keen. The eagle soars at heights where other birds are not able to breathe. The eagle operates at the highest level.

The eagle even makes love in the air; that ensures it only mates with its own species. It never risks partnering with chickens, for example, because, of course, the chicken cannot fly that high. It's not that the chicken doesn't want to; it's just not designed to—its body is too big and its wings are too short. And flap all it wants, the chicken goes five feet in the air and then back down to the ground.

When the eagle spreads its wings, it uses the wind to increase its velocity. So, the greater the storm, the higher the eagle flies, for the storm pushes the eagle higher and higher into the air.

"My God, look at the eagle fly!" exclaimed the little boy. He watched the eagle, first with his own eyes, then through the lenses of his binoculars, the eagle an elegant moving speck. Mesmerized, he watched the winged wonder ascend, circle, glide, and maneuver.

Suddenly the eagle swooped down to the ground like a torpedo. He snatched something and took it back up into the air. The boy couldn't see what it was. And then, oh God, it was a *National Geographic* moment, the eagle went higher and higher and higher and then stopped. The eagle appeared suspended in midair, as if it had been shot.

Now the eagle was falling, as the little boy looked on, confused. This time, the lion of flying creatures was not diving down with aim or focus, it was plummeting, flapping and falling, flapping and falling.

Finally it disappeared from sight. The boy thought, *Did somebody shoot the eagle? I didn't hear a gun. I must find out. I can't go home until I know what happened to the eagle.*

He had to walk a couple of miles to find the eagle, and when he did, there lay nine feet of wings stretched out, helpless. The eagle was lying down, nose in the dirt. It was dead.

The boy kneeled next to the eagle, and sobbed.

What killed the eagle?

Cautiously, he turned the eagle over. There, affixed to the great bird's chest was a weasel—one of the lowliest of common ground critters. This ordinary weasel had bitten through the regal chest, into the heart of the eagle.

Now I see what happened to the eagle, the boy thought. *He picked up something that he wouldn't let go of.* Then, he cried to the dead eagle, "Eagle, you were stronger than the weasel! The weasel could never hurt you if you didn't pick it up and hold on to that old weasel."

In the course of your flight of repositioning yourself, if

you don't drop some things, you'll come crashing down like the eagle. Have you picked up some bad habits, some less than ideal companions, something that's eating at you? Have you picked up something that is stopping you from living your life to the fullest, blocking you from scaling to heights unknown, and preventing you from doing what you were created to do? If you don't drop it, it will bring you down.

What's eating at *your* heart?

The thing that is holding you cannot hold you if you don't hold it. You're stronger than it is. You've been worried or insecure or stressed out or broken or hurting for a long time. You've hidden the weasel and covered for the weasel and never let anybody see the weasel. You've nurtured the weasel and kept the weasel alive because sometimes the weasel was the only company you had. But to make this next move in life, to go to the next level, to reach the next dimension, you can't go any higher with the weasel.

You're an eagle. You were built to fly. You were built to love and be loved, to touch and be touched, to think, to create, to participate. Whom did you pick, or what did you pick up, that has got you living among chickens when you were called to soar like an eagle? Somewhere in your life is a weasel that is eating at you—a weakness, fear, insecurity, vulnerability. Drop the weasel, drop the weasel. Hurry up and drop the weasel before it eats the heart out of your thinking.

Do you want to see the top of the mountains? Do you want to spread your wings and fly through the clouds? Do you want to feel the cool breeze blowing across your face? Do you want to soar so high that the world will know you were here? What do you want? What do you *want* to do with the life you have left? What are you *going* to do with the life that you have left? Are you going to stay in the chicken coop, or are you going to spread your wings and fly?

Spread your wings and let the storms of life lift you up. Reposition yourself.

This is your moment, this is your time, this is your day, this is your hour. Go for it. Position, reposition, switch, shift, change, do what you need to do to get those wings open. Live your life; drop your weasel and go for it. You were meant to fly. Get out of the cage, spread your wings.

What would you do if money were no object? What would you do if fear couldn't stop you? Where would you go if you could fly? What are you going to do with the rest of your life?

God gives you the gift of life and what you do with it is your gift to God.

This Reflection guide is your way to drop the weasel. Its daily reminders, affirmations, thought questions, and passages for reflection will reinforce what you learn in *Reposition Yourself*. You are getting ready to drop the things that have limited you and held you back and stopped you from reaching your fullest potential.

My prayer for you is, *"Father, I thank you for my brothers and sisters. I thank you for how they've gone so far, even carrying what they've been carrying. It's amazing that they got as far as they got, carrying what they're carrying, but God, I come to you asking that my brothers and my sisters would drop whatever does so easily beset them. That they would drop it right now and spread those big beautiful wings into the air and use the storms they've been through to take them to the next level."*

Now you say: *"Good-bye, weasel! I drop you from my life. I drop you from my mind. I drop you from my spirit. I drop you from my finances. I drop you from my business. I drop you from my marriage. I drop you from my ministry. Good-bye, weasel, good-bye. I am going to live my life without limits."*

Introduction

One of the things that moved me to write this Reflection book is that I run into so many people who are stuck. They're not doing badly. They are just stuck in a stage in life where they are not really happy anymore. Sometimes it takes people years to notice that they are not happy, because they are so busy. Before you know it, five, ten, fifteen, twenty years have passed by and you say, "I'm not living life to its fullest. I'm not doing what I want to do."

I wrote *Reposition Yourself* to say to you that just because you started in a certain way doesn't mean you have to end that way. You can change your life and reposition your career, your personal relationships, your ministry, your business, whatever it is you need to tweak.

Every day is important to you; live each day to the fullest. You have permission to change and grow. You learn some things at thirty that you didn't know at eighteen. You know more at fifty than you did at thirty-five. This guide is your resource to take all that you've learned and use it to shift gears and reposition yourself, armed with all of your failures and successes. You learn as much from your failures as you do from your successes. You can reposition yourself and change how your story ends.

You can reposition yourself regardless of your age, regardless of your circumstance. It doesn't matter if you have to start over. Start anew if you have to. You can better yourself if you face the truth, confront yourself. Self-intervention, self-confrontation is very, very important. Bring yourself to the point where you ask, "Am I really living life to the fullest?"

This is not about wealth. You can be wealthy and still be miserable. It's very important to live life fully at whatever stage of life or circumstance you're in. For example, if you're somebody who has a five-bedroom house and you have four kids, but now the kids are gone and you're just holding on to things because that's the way it was, you know that you are in another season of life, a different season than when you bought the house. I'm not here to tell you what you should want at each season. That's your business. I am telling you that you had better ask yourself what you want in this season of your life and go for it. Reposition yourself, and go for it.

How to Use This Book

Reflection is important as you reposition yourself. You must think through your plans and actions carefully. And first, you must think about yourself in a new way.

This book is designed to be read one Reflection at a time and thought about, over and over again. Its three Rs—Reflect, Ruminate, Remember—are a memory device intended to help you embrace, absorb, and apply the message of my book *Reposition Yourself*.

The Reflection numbers are for convenience only. Read the Reflections in the order that fits your need. Skip ones that don't; come back to them another time. Let the book draw you back to the pages that you need as you need them.

Reflect on the personal statement, perhaps even memorize it.

Ruminate on the brief text passage. It's meant for you to ponder. My hope is that it will spur your own thinking about your specific situation. Use it as a yardstick for your own self-examination.

Remember the short summary statement and use it as you move to reposition yourself!

Reflection 1

Reflect

Be honest. Denial is how I get stuck.

Ruminate

We are afraid to really confront the truth. Let me share what happened to me after my mother passed. There is something even deeper than loss about your mom and your dad dying. You realize that there is no generation between you and death.

While I was standing at the casket, looking at my mother—the last of my parents to pass—I thought, "There is nobody left to be in the box but you." Suddenly I was completely uncovered and here is the frightening question I had to ask myself: "What do you want to do with the rest of your life?" I had never asked myself that before. I wasn't sure of the answer. Suppose I don't want to preach? I don't mean to think more highly of myself than I ought to, but I think that more would just shake the nation.

That is why we don't ask the question "What do I want to do with the rest of my life?" Because it opens up the Pandora's box of life.

Maybe you don't want to be married. You are afraid. You are afraid where the answer might take you, so you stick your head in the sand and don't ask the question. But you have to ask the question to be authentic to yourself. You have to have an honest conversation with yourself where you can begin to say, "I need to shift some things to make myself happier. I'm under too much stress. This is not important to me. I don't really need that anymore."

Remember

I can shift my life around and make it work for me, so I can live life to the fullest.

Reflection 2

Reflect

I feel guilty about changing.

Ruminate

We all feel guilty about changing. We were taught to be faithful and loyal. We are afraid to change anything that might indicate we're not a good person. Our parents taught us to get a good job and stay there. Get benefits and work until you retire or die. Get your gold watch. Meet somebody, marry, stay with him (or her), no matter what. (Some kind of man beats no man at all.) They taught us to stand and take it. If we change anything—career, where we live, move out of a bad relationship—we feel like maybe we are not good people.

Parents prepare children for the world the parents know. Children, when they become adults, inevitably live in a totally different world. Parents prepare children for the world, but the world changes.

It is hard to leave behind the teachings you were raised to live by, but in order to reposition yourself, you might have to unlearn some of those lessons. You might have to look at the world with new eyes. You must see the world as it is *now*. It isn't the world of your mother and father, your grandmother and grandfather. You can do what they couldn't. Their shackles are not your shackles. You can have what they couldn't have. Their lack of opportunity and oppression is not your lack of opportunity and oppression. Being faithful and loyal to outdated mind-sets and those who hold them can block you from repositioning yourself.

Remember

Guilt imposed on me by others is unhealthy.

Reflection 3

Reflect

Take the limits off!

Ruminate

Let's teach our daughters to dream and our sons to think. We can take the limits off our situation. Teach children not to color inside the lines, because the lines are what somebody else drew. Say to yourself, "I'm not going to stay inside the lines anymore—the career lines, the relationship lines, the where-I-can-live lines, the what-I-can-read lines, the how-I-talk lines, the wear-the-latest styles and hairdo lines, even the place-of-worship lines. Give me a blank piece of paper and let me create my own life, because I'm too creative to be bogged down by the lines that somebody else drew."

A lot of people are so busy trying to determine what is

holding them back that they can't devote themselves to making the changes they need to make to get ahead. They don't know where racism ends and poverty begins; when you're broke, you can't be sure which thing is holding you back. If you were down in the Gulf when the floods came, maybe you don't know whether you were left behind because you are poor or because you are black. If I'm drowning, it doesn't make any difference whether you left me because I'm black or because I'm poor. But if I have a truck, I can drive out of here. If I have a boat, I can float out of here. If I have a plane ticket, I can fly out. Money gives you options and when you don't have any options you get left behind.

Ignore the lines. They're there—yes. Lines of race, gender, class, and a host of "isms" that will make you, if you allow them, live less than your full potential. Yes, the lines are drawn, but you can get a new sheet of paper. You can reposition yourself to draw your own life.

Remember

What are the limits I have the power right now to remove from my life?

Reflection 4

Reflect

Living my life without limitations means I put serious limitations on my personal spending. I will learn to manage my resources, regardless of what size they are.

Ruminate

Understand that a lot of the financial pathology in the black community results from slavery. Think about it. We worked for food, not money. So our ancestors in this country didn't learn how to handle money. When we were freed by the Emancipation Proclamation, we had the lowest-paying jobs or were sharecroppers who never saw any money from our labor.

In 150 years, we have climbed the economic ladder rapidly, despite what could have been absolutely insurmountable obstacles. Now we earn money! Over the next three years about two hundred billion dollars will come into the African-American community alone. We are very close to one trillion dollars of disposable income, in the African-American community!

When funds get into the hands of people who have no experience with money or who have not been trained to handle it, you know what they do? They spend it. So African-Americans have become the nation's largest spenders. Huge consumers, not investors. We are spending our money on stuff that depreciates, while we are wearing it and driving it. (*Depreciates* means goes down in value with time.) We've got shoes. We've got dresses and hats and coats.

This is not only true in the black community. Sadly, inexperience with money and poor financial training affects Americans across race, and even class. We *all* spend too much, consuming what we do not need. We save too little, if at all. We plan shortsightedly, and with the wrong goals. Few of us invest. This is not just a black issue; there are broke and broken white folks. Just because people are white, doesn't mean that they are well off. There are broken folks in every community.

We must *all* learn to plan, invest, save, build wealth, create value, and pass it down to our children from generation to generation. We must use our money to acquire what escalates in value. (*Appreciates* means gets more and more valuable over time.)

Know the questions to ask and what to talk about, when it comes to money. Watch out for subprime rates and adjustable rate mortgages that are causing folks to lose homes; rent-to-own plans; quick check cashing and tax return operations because they know you want your money quick and you want it now and they are charging you for it.

Remember

Credit is probably the cause of a lot of my misery.

Reflection 5

Reflect

One of the first things I need to do to reposition myself is to get out of debt.

Ruminate

It's very important that we put first things first. I'm not against having nice things. I'm against not having your priorities in place. I'm against investing in your need to look important, driving Bentleys up in front of the projects. I'm against brand-name clothing on children who are flunking out of school. To go forward in life, young people need books and technology and learning tools, not expensive sneakers. I'm against buying lavish furniture for rented apartments. I'm against paying rent your whole life rather than paying off a mortgage, then getting old, getting evicted, and having no place to stay. Home ownership is the beginning of wealth building. My mother told me, you are not a man until you own property; that put feet on me to get my name on a deed, so I could feel like I was somebody. Even the Bible teaches, possess the land.

Women are breaking through the glass ceiling, going to another dimension in terms of earning, but we've got to train them to stop spending all they earn, and borrowing more on credit cards. Start investing. Start producing something. Start owning something. Start developing something.

Most people are in debt; most don't even know their credit score. They haven't even checked. Or, if they know it, and it's poor, they accept it like it is a cancer: "I got bad credit," they'll say, like "I got leukemia."

Debt is a curable disease.

I myself had bad credit. My credit was whack. My car was repossessed. My lights were turned off. My water was cut off. I was cured!

Being challenged financially is very curable, but you've got to have a plan. You have to have a strategy. In the book, I show you the cure.

Good credit is actually the making of a good name for yourself! The Bible teaches the importance of a good name.

That is all good credit is. It is your good name with the business community. Restore your good name by taking one of the first steps for repositioning yourself—getting out of debt and establishing good credit.

Remember

Prosperity is not real if it's based on debt.

Reflection 6

Reflect

Subconsciously, I have a mentality that if I become really successful, I'll experience a negative aftertaste.

Ruminate

You escaped. You broke loose and have some measure of success. You live with the knowledge that some are thinking or even saying to your face, "We'll burn your 'black card' in a minute if you become too successful." You've heard that little voice in your head.

This is not only a "black" thing. Substitute whatever phrase the little voice says when it nags *you*! When we begin to change, some around us begrudge our growth and success.

I'm not preaching the "prosperity gospel." The word *gos-*

pel has only one meaning. To the Christian, there is only one Gospel: God's grace extended through the death, burial, and resurrection of our Lord Jesus. We must never confuse the benefits with a payday. God offers us eternal life, not everlasting use of a Rolls-Royce! Yet, somehow, if a preacher even mentions earning, spending, saving, or investing money, folks immediately apply the prosperity gospel label. Jesus taught on every aspect of life.

Remember

I choose the kind of person I become as I grow more and more successful. I can help others, especially those I love, handle their feelings that arise as I become successful, but I cannot stunt my growth because of them.

Reflection 7

Reflect

I can acquire the good things in life and still be a good human being, one who pleases God.

Ruminate

God doesn't mind you having things. God minds things having you. God expects those who prosper to appreciate that their ability to prosper comes from God, and to learn how to manage those resources. You are able to do things like dig wells in drought-stricken areas of Kenya. You can't do that if you're broke.

The world reacted to poor people in the Gulf when Katrina hit, as if it was a big revelation that there were poor people who had no means of getting out. There are poor people in every city. God expects us to help and train them. The church is one of the few institutions that reaches masses of people, one at a time.

Part of repositioning yourself is moving yourself to a position where you can share and help others more. As you grow and achieve, your success directly and intentionally benefits others. You become a conduit for God's blessings.

Remember

If I'm committed to doing good, and serving God, my possessions serve a greater good.

Reflection 8

Reflect

I can reposition myself, achieve success, and still remain humble.

Ruminate

Someone said to me, "You're this kid from the hills, from the coal mines! You preach and teach, make movies, write books." And then she asked, "How do you get it all accomplished and with such a high degree of success, yet stay humble?"

I laughed. I'm far too busy to dwell on my success or rest on any laurels I may have. I am in a fight to share with people as much as I can. Preaching is one avenue, but sometimes preaching does not allow me to show people the chemistry behind what I do. When I write a book, I can provide details. Making a movie allows me to impart in a different way.

Humility is easier to maintain when you live life with a strategy. When you have a strategy, achievement means accomplishing a set goal; it's not about self.

I am living my life strategically. I want to hand the plan to the next guy. I don't have anything to prove. I've already done what I set out to do. I want to see somebody else get the ball. It's not about me anymore. It's about my kids—my sons, my daughters. I am very passionate about my children. More than anything I want to see my children succeed. I mean *more than anything*. It means everything in the world to me. And then, to see my spiritual children succeed. I am trying to hand off the baton and say, "Look, I didn't have anything—just a rag and a rock. And I made something of it. I give you what I've made, with God's grace. Now you take it and run with it."

Having a strategy to reposition yourself—whether its goal is, like mine, for your family or some other greater good—will help keep you humble as you achieve greater and greater success.

Remember

Humility doesn't come from humble circumstances. Successes can build character. Humility is an aspect of good character.

Reflection 9

Reflect

Understanding myself is the beginning of branding myself.

Ruminate

A brand just lets people know what to expect when they come to you.

People have heard this term "branding yourself" applied to members of the hip-hop culture—Diddy, Jay-Z—and the younger generation. When you see Tyler Perry's name on a DVD jacket, movie marquee, on the program for a stage production, or hosting an event, you smile to yourself knowing that he's going to entertain you. Each of these successful individuals has followed his bliss professionally, so that who they are becomes synonymous with what they bring to everything they touch. They are recognizable and understandable.

They have identity and create and fulfill expectations. This is what a brand really is all about.

If I say, "We do chicken right," you recognize KFC. That means don't drive up to the window looking for a steak and a baked potato! They have branded their business: fried chicken is what they do.

This is a principle—it applies whether it's a business or a date, and it has nothing to do with being rich or famous.

To create your personal brand, you must understand who you are. Be able to articulate who you are. When you present yourself to people your "brand" is saying, "This is what you get when you get me." This is what I bring to the table.

It's easier to date successfully when you have branded yourself. You know and reveal openly who you are. Your behavior says, "If you take me to be your husband, this is what you're going to get when you get me." When you go on an interview, your brand is saying, "Here's what I bring to the job."

Remember

My brand is a promise I know I can deliver because I understand myself.

Reflection 10

Reflect

My mission statement is . . .

Ruminate

Everyone needs to develop a personal mission statement. It is a simple declaration of who you are and what you are about.

With this in mind, write your personal mission statement. It can be as simple as: I'm T.D. Jakes and I want to educate, empower, and entertain everyone I encounter.

Start by answering some questions: What do you want to be about? What is your vision, your purpose, your mission? Are you demonstrating who you really are? Are you delivering what you really care about?

Are you trapped in circumstances where you're expected to deliver what is not even in you? So often we try to be someone we're not. Due to pressure we exert on ourselves or the pressure from our families, spouses, friends, and co-workers, we find ourselves attempting to deliver what is not authentic to who we are and what we're about.

A mission statement cuts through all the expectation and says, "I am _____ and my life is to _____ ." Make sure your mission statement defines you for you and clarifies what your life purpose is, as you see it.

Remember

I continue to grow and change. My goals will expand. My definition of myself and life purpose in my mission statement is broad enough to accommodate my life without limits!

Reflection 11

Reflect

I am not defined by the label others put on me.

Ruminate

Time magazine, CNN, and others have called me America's greatest preacher, and that is all really flattering, but I still don't like labels because labels limit. The implication is that that is all I am. People say, "You're a preacher, what are you doing, doing so-and-so? You are a preacher." They put a period where God put a comma.

Labels limit you and they generally misrepresent you. When people say, "You are this or that," they are saying what they know you to be. They don't know the whole you.

Let's take Queen Latifah, for example. She comes on the stage, baseball cap turned around backward, doing rap music. Next time you see her, she's all dressed up, at the Oscars for a stunning acting performance. Look again, she's doing a talk show. Blink and she's writing a children's book. You blink again, she's put out a jazz CD. What is she saying? "There is more in me than any label can convey."

There is more in you, too, I guarantee you. There is more in you than how people define you. When they label you, they limit you.

Those who met me forty years ago labeled me, but must I be that for forty years? Even those who labeled me ten years ago didn't grasp the whole me. Yes, I do preach. But there is other stuff in me. I want to build. I want to own my own business. I may want to draw. I want to paint. No labels for me! I want to do everything I can do while I'm living. When I wake up in the morning I want to get out of bed and do something fresh and exciting.

Remember

No label is definitive enough for me!

Reflection 12

Reflect

I don't have to become bored.

Ruminate

Do something fresh! Read a book. Take up a hobby or a sport. Learn a language. Change!

This is how we lose our marriages. You're boring. You're a good wife. You're just boring. You're a good husband. You're just boring. You've been with him/her a year or ten years or you fill in the blank. There is nothing to discover. There is nothing new to find. You don't read anything, you don't have anything fresh to say.

Make yourself interesting again so that people can find a new woman in the old woman, a new man in the old man. What often happens to married people that makes them prone to affairs is somebody comes along and sees something in your old man or your old woman that you overlooked. Start looking for a new man in the old man. Start looking for a new woman in the old woman. It's in there and we love people who help us get it out of us. We love preachers who help us get it out of us. We love companions who help us mine the treasure that we have inside.

Remember

Boredom indicates I need to reposition myself.

Reflection 13

Reflect

What I did for the first ten or twenty years of my life may not be the only gifting that I have.

Ruminate

We no longer live in an economy where a person is trained for one career and works at it for life. The concept of starting at a company when one is young and staying there until retirement is almost laughable these days. Employees keep their resumes handy and jump at new opportunities. They are not loyal to companies and companies certainly aren't loyal to employees. Massive layoffs, downsizings, and exporting jobs are the rule.

As challenging as this world-of-work reality may be, it is good news for those of us who understand the need to regularly reposition ourselves. It allows us to look for our giftings, rather than rest on our laurels. We can make bold changes in our working choices, explore new facets of ourselves, learn new skills, adapt to other environments, make new friends.

The beauty of repositioning yourself is the chance to re-invent yourself. And no matter how much you reinvent yourself, you cannot exhaust God's giftings in you. You were so marvelously made that you will never discover them all!

Remember

Repositioning myself will allow me to see what else God has inside of me.

Reflection 14

Reflect

Relationships, family, and the people in my life who got me to where I am are important.

Ruminate

Often with success, you become the star of the play of your life and your family and friends become walk-on extras or people you leave behind. That's not true success. Bring them along. We have the tendency to take our families for granted, and then we foolishly think we have outgrown them or they haven't kept up with us. It is our responsibility to make certain that that gap does not occur.

I talk to so many men who feel as if they can't relate to their wives anymore, and sometimes it is the wives who helped push them. It is the wife who helped work to get the man back in or through school. It's the wife who did the hard work and the grunt work. Then he grows up, goes up, and feels embarrassed by her. He doesn't want to take her to the meeting. She doesn't do, look, talk, relate, whatever, the way he wishes she would. And with the breaking of the glass ceiling for women, this is becoming more and more true in the reverse.

Repositioning yourself involves repositioning your family and friends.

Always acknowledge your spouse. Let people know, "This woman (or man) is important to me. I wouldn't be who I am today without her (him)." It gives value to the person.

It is hard not to grow apart when you function in one world and your spouse functions in another. You're busy. You don't have a lot of time. You look around, years have gone by; and all of a sudden you have nothing to talk about other than the business of marriage—"You picking up the kids today?" "No, you pick them up." "You taking the trash out?" "I'll take it out." All that's left is the business of marriage; the relationship has crystallized.

But you can avoid this and reverse it. Come home and share your experiences with your family or your close friends.

Every time I have a new experience, I want my wife and children to share that experience, so we don't grow apart.

Remember

In order to make sure that I don't leave my family and friends behind, to bridge that gap, to close it, to make that connection, I must communicate.

Reflection 15

Reflect

I have to inspire and motivate my children to make sure that I don't leave them behind.

Ruminate

One of the mistakes I realize I've made is being so busy trying to get there myself that I didn't recognize that my kids need the same thing I do—fellowship with other young people who think like I'm rearing them to think, not people who are draining them.

We have to educate our young people to reposition themselves against the expectations of youth culture.

I took my family on a business cruise for influential African-American families, and it was there that I recognized the importance of creating a social environment that was

conducive to the vision I had for my children. I thought I was
going to network on the cruise, but I ended up spending
more time observing my children. I overheard them talking
about college. I was happy to notice them speaking about
business and law degrees, as opposed to the normal teenage
chatter. I realized then that my training was not enough;
I needed to use strategic socialization to provide them with
an environment that positioned them socially for where I
wanted them to go in life.

Remember

My children don't experience the person I am in the world of
work, and other places outside our home, unless I take them
with me and share that part of myself at home.

Reflection 16

Reflect

It is boring always to be the top person.

Ruminate

You probably live in a world where everybody is making a withdrawal from you. They want something from you 24/7. "I need you to do this and would you do that. Can you come over here and do that?" If everybody is making a withdrawal and nobody is making a deposit, guess what, you're going to be bankrupt in a minute. I tell people all the time, if you live in a circle, in an orbit where you are the smartest person in that orbit you're in the wrong orbit. You've outgrown that orbit. You need to transition to the next level where there is somebody in the room who makes you study again, who makes you a little bit nervous, who makes you have to read up because you're a little bit intimidated. That is a great feeling. That is life. That is pizzazz. That is passion.

Remember

Iron sharpens iron. —Proverbs 27:17 (KJV)

Reflection 17

Reflect

With repositioning myself will come more pressure, but I can manage it.

Ruminate

I have been asked how I handle so much pressure—the comparisons to Billy Graham, even Bill Gates. I am a very, very strategic person. I live according to my plans, not by outside pressure. I hardly ever do anything without a reason. I am a big thinker. I try to plan what is most important to me.

I never get to the end of the day and finish. I've learned that it's OK to go to bed with work undone. It's going to carry over. One day I'm going to die with work undone. I'm not going to stay up any longer than I choose to because of pressure.

I will see further than I will ever go. That's because I am a visionary. One day I'm going to climb up to the top of a mountain and look over to a land that I won't be able to go to, but all those who heard me will cross over. And I'm OK with that.

Great people never reach everything they see. You just keep walking and walking and one day God snatches you home and everybody who was walking with you continues to march in that rhythm. Martin Luther King, Jr., said, "I might not get there with you but I've seen the other side." Every person who is a visionary can see further can they will go because God thinks in generations. David gathered the cedars of Lebanon but Solomon built the temple. One day you are going to gather something that only your kids can finish. So don't view the challenges that will inevitably come with repositioning yourself as pressure, but as a big vision, of which you will accomplish your part, and leave the rest for the next person.

Remember

There is some Moses in us all.

Reflection 18

Reflect

Delay is not a denial.

Ruminate

How do you tell the difference between delay and denial? How do you know whether it's God saying, "No, that's not for you," or God saying, "Be patient. Now is not the time. It will come later"?

I leave it up to God to say, "No." The same God who opens doors, closes doors. But you can rest assured I'm going to knock on that sucker real hard. It's God's business to shut doors and if God shuts them, I can accept that, but it's my business to knock. I'm going to knock on them until I understand a definite "no."

Remember

I rejoice as much at "no" as I do at "yes" because "no" just frees me to go to another door and start knocking on it.

Reflection 19

Reflect

Healing is harder than hiding, but things can turn out the way I want if I'm willing to heal and not hide.

Ruminate

Think honestly about the issues that may be stopping you from reaching your goals and living your life to the fullest. You might even ask a trusted friend to tell you the truth.

None of us welcomes regret into our lives. We want to live to the fullest, spiritually, financially, and relationally. Yet we often settle for less than the best life we could live. Lulled into sleep by a sense of apathetic compliance, we accept as limitations situations that could be transcended.

Remember

Pain has a purpose when it is for healing, rather than hiding.

Reflection 20

Reflect

Living without limits means constantly changing boundaries.

Ruminate

My life has constantly changed and evolved in response to the events, people, and opportunities around me. I have been divinely blessed by my Creator. But I've also made deliberate attempts to grow, to position myself to receive, and to reposition myself to receive more.

I have failed and tried again, many times, before making significant progress toward my goals. My mistakes were also my lessons. As I gained in experience and did not allow my past mistakes to bind and gag me, the boundaries established in my own mind for how far I can go were pushed outward. I found the keys to leading a life without limits.

Remember

Mistakes and failures expand my limits, just as successes do, if I learn from them.

Reflection 21

Reflect

Success is a direct consequence of wanting a more abundant life and working hard to earn it.

Ruminate

Like wading through the mud puddles of life toward the beckoning sea, delays, setbacks, and challenges have often compelled me to revise my own definition of success and prosperity. I understand that prosperity is more than the trinkets of excess we use as icons of accomplishment and self-worth in our culture. I have come to realize that prosperity is built upon progress, and that progress is measured in relation to that point from which we started.

Remember

My success is measured by how far I've come from where I began, not how much farther I have to go to reach my goals.

Reflection 22

Reflect

I recover from lost opportunities with experience to make another attempt.

Ruminate

The sad memories of a lost opportunity have made many people bitter the rest of their lives. Often it is not the fatigue of the Olympic competitor that is debilitating as much as it is the feeling that if he had lunged farther, or pushed harder, he might have been holding the golden cup of victory as opposed to the bottled water of defeat.

Remember

If I have not been able to turn opportunity into a prize, I certainly can turn it into a lesson.

Reflection 23

Reflect

Faith, work, and responsibility make dreams realities.

Ruminate

Faith is the substance of whatever it is that we hope for. The important thing is that we teach that faith is connected to good works and responsibility. When we teach that faith is all one has to have, we teach a belief in magic.

Remember

I direct my hope toward building my dreams instead of hoping my dreams will build themselves.

Reflection 24

Reflect

I can only correct what I am willing to confront.

Ruminate

Confrontation isn't something that I enjoy. But I have learned over the years to say what has to be said and face what has to be faced. Many choose to live in a perpetual state of denial rather than risk the hard work that is needed to confront issues, weaknesses, and inconsistencies in others—and in themselves.

The anxiety we experience when we confront is much to be preferred to the deadening of our emotions that goes with denial.

Do you have the courage to face the dark, silently sinister enemy that may be lurking inside of you? Do you have the courage to confront yourself?

Remember

Often the "enemy" is actually the "inner me."

Reflection 25

Reflect

Love always wins.

Ruminate

Perhaps you're familiar with the process known as intervention. Frequently used for cases of abuse of such sub-
stances as alcohol and drugs, as well as for various addictions
to unhealthy behaviors, intervention is a valuable tool for
helping the person who has destructive behavior see the pat-
terns of his life and the effects they are having on those
around him.

When conducted in a spirit of love and encouragement,
the intervention can save the life of the addict and reawaken
her to a world filled with opportunities for health and well-

ness. It is simply amazing how love can win over obsessions, addictions, or anything else that is having an adverse effect.

Remember

Love can be a tremendous deterrent to destructive behavior; it provides the support needed for change.

Reflection 26

Reflect

Repositioning myself involves becoming vulnerable enough to others to ask for their feedback and trusting that they will lovingly tell me the truth, as they see it.

Ruminate

Ask your spouse or partner, your kids, perhaps your best friend, siblings, parents, co-workers, or pastor for feedback. Use their comments to determine how you need to reposition yourself. Ask them about your talents and what they see as your ambition. There are many people in your immediate circle who may be watching you live your life in ways that are far beneath your real potential and true character. Ask those people what they've noticed and been witnessing in your life.

Remember

In the multitude of counsellors there is safety. —Proverbs 11:14 (KJV)

Reflection 27

Reflect

Action is my simple antidote to apathy.

Ruminate

Apathy has caused many to withhold the best parts of themselves from the world—from their family, friends, work, church, community. It dulls one's gifting. We each bear the responsibility to break addiction to apathy and unleash the passion of our life without limits.

Remember

A decision to reposition myself is a choice to lift my life out of the realm of the ordinary and into the spectacular realm of extraordinary possibility thinking.

Reflection 28

Reflect

I am willing to fight.

Ruminate

You can have a better life. The question is, Are you willing to fight for it? Like an alcoholic recovering from the throes of his addiction, are you willing to fight the urge to settle for less and to endure the hard work required to reposition yourself? Are you willing to fight to reposition yourself so that you're no longer settling and instead are satisfying the various parts of who you really are?

Remember

The time has never been better to create an impact on the world around me.

Reflection 29

Reflect

I am willing to fight with my eyes open.

Ruminate

I have never forgotten the invaluable life lesson I learned as a boy from a bully named Harold. One day after school we had words about something. We had traded insults back and forth after the bell rang but waited until we were almost home to actually scuffle. We punched and rolled, swinging fists like prizefighters on pay-per-view. I sweated and cursed, screamed and swung, while he punched me in the eye and the lip. Angrier than ever, I became even more misguided in my efforts to fight back.

I sustained a fairly uncontested "beat-down." Harold beat me so badly that when my father came home that evening, he got down on his knees and gave me my first lesson in self-defense. Dad, who was my superhero at the time, had me demonstrate my stance and technique. After observing me for a moment, he chuckled and said, "Son, your big mistake is that your arms are flailing out there like you're imitating a windmill. And your bigger mistake is that your eyes are closed, like you don't want to watch someone kick your tail!"

Often our busy schedules are full of activities that are like those empty punches, that don't connect with anything of substance. Sometimes our eyes are closed to the realities necessary to fulfill our true potential.

Remember

I must fight strategically for the prizes I long to enjoy.

Reflection 30

Reflect

The danger of traditional thinking is stagnation.

Ruminate

The wisdom of our elders could have been great for their times. But we need a progressive and continual reassessment, in order to avoid the pitfall of applying an antiquated, ineffective ideology. To survive in the highly technical and postindustrial age that you and I live in today, we have to update our personal philosophy. Our parents and ancestors have laid a great foundation, for which I am eternally grateful. But it is dangerous to build additions to a house that was constructed for a climate very different from the present one. Yet subconsciously we often stay with the inherited framework and never make any advance into contemporary progressive thinking.

Remember

As he thinketh in his heart, so is he. —Proverbs 23:7 (KJV)

Reflection 31

Reflect

Mistakes are lessons.

Ruminate

Learning from past mistakes is part of repositioning your-self. I talk a lot about mistakes because so many of us are car-rying the burden of mistakes, and it limits our vision of what we can have, be, and do.

Learn from them, instead of repeating them. Regret them, be deeply sorry for them, apologize for them, make amends for them, mourn the losses they result in. These are all healthy responses to our mistakes.

But do not allow mistakes to make your life a treadmill of activity after activity, where you are simply running in place, doing chore after chore, duty after duty. If you are expending constant motion only to stay in place at best, you may have boxed yourself in by what you feel you "should do" because of past mistakes. Even the brightest, most intelligent, highly successful people make decisions that they later regret. Repositioning to change direction from past mistakes is not easy, but it can be done.

Remember

No mistake—no matter how large, costly, embarrassing, or painful—can cost me the power to change my life.

Reflection 32

Reflect

The only thing certain about life is that it will change. I embrace life's unexpected changes.

Ruminate

Like a baby developing from stage to stage, life has a way of presenting us with surprises. One moment a job is a wonderful blessing, and a few years later you find yourself standing before an arbitration board with frustration that you never saw coming. One doesn't have to live long to know that even a wonderful relationship, business or personal, often presents challenges that can quickly turn into a conflict resembling the battle of Armageddon! I have seen children who were once confidants and trusted allies turn on their own parents and try to destroy them. I have witnessed lovers who couldn't breathe without hearing each other's heartbeat, later abhor the sound of the other's voice. Even a trusted friend can end up a formidable enemy.

But none of these unexpected changes has to prevent us from repositioning ourselves. Change is to be embraced in ways that move us toward our goals.

Remember

How change *feels* does not determine whether or not I embrace it.

Reflection 33

Reflect

I not only break through barriers, I transform them into resources.

Ruminate

We can convert storms of opposition into wind beneath our
wings. We can use experiences that push us to the wall to
break through barriers and expand our playing field. We can
move beyond the limits of our past mistakes, transforming folly into wisdom, frustration into fuel, and denial into
the detonator of explosive change. The failures of the past
can become battle scars that toughen our hides and make
us more resilient and resourceful moving forward, if we

allow those tender wounds of regret and disappointment to heal.

Remember

Often my greatest barrier is my thinking about my past mistakes.

Reflection 34

Reflect

I cultivate the mind of a champion.

Ruminate

There is a mind-set of the champion that gives him an edge. It is his refusal to accept average or ordinary that puts him in a place of unprecedented distinction. In fact, there is a discipline and training that forever positions the gladiator as the prevailing winner he was meant to be. Once he has been programmed to succeed, he will ultimately rise to his highest and best self because he has been trained to win, conditioned to prevail, and called to be a conqueror. He has been positioned to be a winner, and even if he loses everything, he has that nebulous, seemingly indefinable gift, of landing on his feet in shoes with silver linings.

Remember

The repositioning process begins with understanding how relentless and tenacious I must be in order to prevail over adversity.

Reflection 35

Reflect

Success is intentional.

Ruminate

Do you not know that in a race all the runners run, but only one gets the prize? Run in such a way as to get the prize. Everyone who competes in the games goes into strict training. They do it to get a crown that will not last; but we do it to get a crown that will last forever. Therefore I do not run like a man running aimlessly; I do not fight like a man beating the air. No, I beat my body and make it my slave so that after I have preached to others, I myself will not be disqualified for the prize. —1 Corinthians 9:24–27 (NIV)

The day of competition, the sheer joy of it, is intoxicating. Completing the race is an extremely gratifying feeling, even if you don't win. You discover that the discipline of preparation is itself a personal prize you have given yourself.

Remember

Success—whether spiritual, physical, or financial—is intentional. No one trips across a finish line in the Olympics and says, "Oh, wow! How did I do that?"

Reflection 36

Reflect

Building my personal empowerment arsenal starts with looking honestly at myself.

Ruminate

Every retail business, from shoe stores to supermarkets, has to assess what it actually has in the store compared with what the records indicate should be in the store. Similarly, we must assess what we have in our personal warehouses.

The first step in repositioning yourself is arming yourself with an accurate analysis of your gifts and dedicating your efforts to cultivating the area of your gifting. Fulfilling your purposes for living begins with identifying the areas that give you a sense of satisfaction and well-being. (Most people have more than one gifting and purpose and may explore them simultaneously, or decide at some later date to go after a dream that was put on hold for a while.) You must have the courage and tenacity to see that abstract fantasy becomes concrete reality in your life.

Remember

I must correctly assess gifts—what I have in my personality that can empower me as I reposition myself.

Reflection 37

Reflect

I dance to the beat of my own drum.

Ruminate

Most of us are forever living our lives dancing to the beat of someone else's drum. I have had to learn as a parent that I can influence but I cannot control my children's choices. At times I have sincerely, but wrongly, tried to relive my life vicariously through my children. And I'm not alone. Many parents have taken their influence to an extreme and put their children in a lifelong prison of trying to live up to a mother's or father's expectations.

Or what about those of us who allow our competitive tendency to compel us toward what we actually do not want, just in order to prove a point to someone else? Their opinion becomes the barometer of our accomplishment.

We must be honest with ourselves and listen to that voice within us, pay attention to what makes our minds race and our pulses skip. If this self-exam makes you squirm, I encourage you to look at what's making you uncomfortable. Your dream need not be lofty. Your goal may appear quite commonplace. There is no shame in being a janitor if you do it with pride, dignity, and a sense of fulfilling your true purpose. I know because my father was one.

Remember

The first step in taking inventory is to be real with myself about who I am and what I really want.

Reflection 38

Reflect

I equip myself with the right tools to fulfill my dreams.

Ruminate

The right tools help me perform each task along the way as I reposition myself. What are these tools?

Some are the navigational tools, the people who influence and guide us and the institutions and systems that do so. Sometimes a mentor is a navigational influence. Sometimes parents can be navigational influences. Prayer, talking with God, always assists with navigation.

Other tools we need to succeed in repositioning ourselves are clarity about the season of life we are in, conviction about the contribution we are making with our lives, awareness of our own frailties, and flexibility to adapt to unexpected setbacks.

Hard work, relentless commitment, debt reduction, small investments, home ownership, and education are effective tools for long-term financial health, which is a key part of re-positioning.

Remember

My arsenal of tools is not limited to my own strengths. I surround myself with people who lend me their tools.

Reflection 39

Reflect

Adopt to adapt.

Ruminate

Ability to adapt to change means we assess the business climate. We utilize past data before investing. We attack or defend with the skillful accuracy of a professional. Adapting means picking up the vocabulary and skills needed for the situation. It means learning the rules of that particular game, the culture of that workplace, the way of relating in that social setting.

It's when in Rome, doing as the Romans do, yet still remaining uniquely you.

Remember

Adopting new ways can unleash who I was meant to be, as I adapt to changing times and new experiences.

Reflection 40

Reflect

I choose state over fate.

Ruminate

The question I had to ask myself in those times when I was sinking in a quicksand of debt, sitting in the dark with no electricity, stuck at home with my car repossessed, and facing a hungry family I had no means to feed, was this: Do I accept this as my fate or simply as a temporary state?

If it is my fate, then I'm finished and I should give up. Fate means it was just meant to be, it's my lot in life.

I answered that it was a state, a temporary state, one that I could, with all diligence, fashion, transform, and resist. I did not succumb to despair, but rather persevered in moving forward. The rest is history.

You are writing your history now. There is no such thing as fate. Fate is a lie. All human beings were created by God with a will. Will means you have power to choose.

Remember

I can't determine the final outcome of my situation, but I *can* choose to accept a situation as my fate or just endure it while I persevere to change it.

Reflection 41

Reflect

Like Joseph, I can live without limits even "in prison."

Ruminate

One of the reasons my heart breaks for the many men and women I have met in prison is that most of them are highly gifted, intelligent, and creative.

The biblical figure Joseph repositioned himself from convict to commissioner. (Read about his life in detail in Genesis chapters 37–40.) He was bound by his circumstances. But he overcame them by using his mind. Joseph was incarcerated, but even there, he found a way to apply his abilities. He repositioned himself in a time of need to provide a service. He used his gifts in order to transcend from the mundane to the miraculous.

Remember

I have the power to move beyond my present prison, even if it involves confronting a degrading, demeaning scenario that has left me feeling uncertain and irrelevant.

Reflection 42

Reflect

Despair is the enemy of vision.

Ruminate

Vision, so crucial to this process of repositioning yourself, is often one of the first powers we lose when despair sets in. Several years ago I met with a gentleman who was running for president in his country. He was discouraged by a lack of finances and felt defeated. I spent a few hours motivating him to believe in himself and his abilities. He thought his problem was lack of finances, but I knew that it was lack of vision. He couldn't recognize where he was. Initially, I think he wanted me to be a campaign contributor, but what I gave him was better than money. I sat with him and helped him locate himself.

Remember

I cannot achieve what I cannot conceive.

Reflection 43

Reflect

I can determine where I am by evaluating what I have accomplished and comparing it with what I dream of achieving.

Ruminate

The idea of life is to get what you see on the inside to happen on the outside. You will know you have it when there is no difference between what you see when you sleep and what you wake up to. It is possible to live your dream, wide awake. The distance between what you dream and what you see is achievable. That achievement is determined by your ability to commit to and engage in what you dream about.

This is not a question of whether you have skills. It is not a matter of possessing a dream. Rather, does the dream possess you? Does it possess you enough to sacrifice?

Remember

Fulfillment is living what I once dreamed about.

Reflection 44

Reflect

To reposition myself, I must go back to "one."

Ruminate

My mother was an educator, and she taught all of us to count before we went to school. Could we count! As little bitty kids, we could count to one hundred, because Mama sat down on the floor and taught us. I had to count to one hundred and I was having some trouble. I couldn't get it. It was too many numbers. Maybe if she had given me a few dozen biscuits to count, I could have gotten those, but I couldn't count to one hundred.

"One, two, three, four, seven. One, two, three, four, six. One, two, three, four, five, six, eight. One, two, three, four, fix, six, seven, nine. Let me do it again—one, two, three, four, five, six, seven, eight, nine, ten!" I said, "Mama, I can count to ten!"

She said, "That's not good enough. You've got to count to one hundred."

"Mama, I can count to ten."

"I want you to count to one hundred."

All of a sudden, I said, "Mama, I don't have to count to one hundred. All I have to do is count to ten because every one of those big numbers is like a ten!" I'd finally gotten it. Mama was proud of me.

And truly, I've have never had to count to one hundred. I'm almost fifty years old; I still haven't had to count to one hundred, or one thousand or a million or a billion or a trillion. All I ever have to do is count to ten because in every one of those numbers are repetitions of ten. One, two, three, four, five, six, seven, eight, nine, ten, *one again* (eleven), twelve, thirteen, fourteen, fifteen, sixteen, seventeen, eighteen, nineteen, twenty, *one again,* two, three, four, five, six, seven, eight, nine, thirty, *one again.*

We get stuck at ten in life. If you're going to go to the next level, you've got to be willing to go back to one again. Do you want to be a big thing on a low level, or are you willing to go back to one again on the next level to move into the next dimension? You might be a ten in your current sphere. To move to higher, you might have to be a *one again*. Go back to one and get a new and exciting revelation of learning. Repeat the process over and over again, each time at a higher and higher, more and more successful level.

Remember

Becoming more and more successful means I start over again and again in life, but each time at a new level, a higher level.

Reflection 45

Reflect

One way I avoid stagnation is not to allow myself to reduce prosperity to success and money.

Ruminate

Progress apart from purpose ends in arrogance.

Success can often make the successful become out of touch with their passion. Truly successful individuals discover that they must unleash their passion in other areas if they are to remain engaged with life and avoid boredom of the soul. They need a fresh challenge.

Remember

I may need to reposition myself, not because my life is not already terrific, but because I need a new adventure.

Reflection 46

Reflect

Whether I'm doing well or not, it's just a season.

Ruminate

Life is a series of cycles. These cycles are referred to as seasons of life. Understanding this "seasonal" truth will help you avoid worry. You will realize that wherever you are, this, too, shall pass. If this is a good season, you won't become over-confident and think you are exempt from a challenging one at some later point. If it's a tough season, you won't allow anyone to give you a prognosis of death. You'll know you can break out. Mentors, parents, and prayer are some seasonal tools that can help you through all seasons.

Remember

I know a cycle is really nothing more than a circle, so I can circle back, only this time, I'll take it to the next level—a level without limits!

Reflection 47

Reflect

I cannot thrive in the wrong environment.

Ruminate

Jesus said, "Save yourself from this untoward generation." You must leave an environment in which you cannot reposition yourself for growth. Many men with good intentions want to come back and change the neighborhood in which they grew up. But be careful, you must be fully aware of what you are facing. If you're aware of what confines you, then you can overcome it. If you can escape it, you can transform it. But you cannot transform what influences you. Face up to this fact squarely.

One thing that helps us to reposition ourselves is to associate with people who are moving in the same direction we are, people who are in our same "neighborhood" regarding their goals. Such people help shape our habits, and our habits help develop our character. Learn the mind-set of champions, the attitude of people who achieve in your chosen field. You will discover yourself developing the lifestyle of a winner simply by associating with those who are what you want to become.

Remember

Environment has much to do with results.

Reflection 48

Reflect

Stop "retro" living!

Ruminate

Most of us are stuck because we live where we are accustomed to living. We cling to places from the past. We hold on to old relationships that retard our progress.

A healthy environment is a place where you can grow, and it must include people who will support and encourage you, challenge and stimulate you.

If you are to reposition yourself successfully, then you must begin today to build a support system that is based not on where you come from, or even what you did wrong, but on where you intend to go.

Do you have the right people around you for where you

are going? Identify those who are right for you and build those relationships. Approach them with humility, as well as confidence, and let them know, by what you say and how you behave around them, that they are significant to your success. (The wrong way to approach them is from a place of neediness.) Ask yourself what you have to offer them, how you can make their lives better. We all love to be around others who both give to and receive from us.

Remember

Just because it *was* does not mean it must *be*.

Reflection 49

Reflect

I will bring my gifts.

Ruminate

Whenever I'm visited by African leaders, they always come with a gift. As you know, Africa is a continent comprising many countries, and within those nations, many peoples. But in the Motherland, giving gifts is common across national and cultural lines. Africans always bring a welcoming gift to those with whom they are meeting, regardless of what they expect the meeting to bring them. Because many are from agricultural backgrounds, they know that you cannot reap where you have not sown, you cannot harvest fruit if you have not planted seeds and fertilized the ground.

    At first I found it confusing, since in our country we typically show up for appointments and meetings empty-handed. Then I began to understand and appreciate this African custom. Proverbs 18:16 (NIV) says the gift opens the way for the giver. For those of us who are repositioning ourselves, this can mean that our skills, talents, and abilities are the gifts we bring to any situation, whether it is work, relationships, or civic and church activity. We come prepared to give the best of ourselves. That is our gift.

Remember

I come to every situation prepared with what I can give of myself, my skills, talents, abilities, knowledge, experience. I always have something to contribute and I offer it freely.

Reflection 50

Reflect

I will hope in the face of adversity.

Ruminate

You don't have to be an oddsmaker in Las Vegas to know how difficult it can be to sustain hope in the face of life's many adversities. No one is immune to the virulent attacks of illness, divorce, unemployment, or loneliness. We all deal daily with the sharp collision of our external realities and our internal aspirations. The result is often a wreck of major proportions that leaves us limping through another day, sore and disjointed, more exhausted and discouraged than we can imagine. Life is not fair. You will have to overcome odds that may be stacked against you.

But you can change the outcome of your life if you will refuse to give up hope.

Remember

Hope is not about the odds. Hope says the odds don't matter.

Reflection 51

Reflect

I throw out the statistics!

Ruminate

You cannot base your life on the so-called "odds" of your demographics. You do not allow others' perceptions and probabilities to define you and decide your destiny. You are the only one who controls your success.

Statistics are not operating laws of the universe, locking you in to some unalterable existence. They are simply a brief snapshot of a group at one point in time. They are no more able to predict your future than that freshman-year photo of you in your high school yearbook—you know, the one where you were having a really bad hair day!

Remember

I am not a statistic. I am a unique, God-created individual with a specific destiny, which I ultimately control.

Reflection 52

Reflect

I take responsibility.

Ruminate

A member of the press asked me whose position I supported on the matter of individual or social responsibility, Michael Eric Dyson's or Bill Cosby's. I asked, in response, that the interviewer take a quarter out of his pocket and examine it. I then asked him which side was the correct side. It was my way of saying that both men's views are valid and significant. They represent opposite sides of the same coin.

Regarding repositioning yourself, though, I must tell you that you are solely responsible for you. You will likely receive support, encouragement, perhaps even mentoring and tangible help as you take your life to the next level. But you can't count on it. You must act as if it all depends on you.

Remember

Life is unfair. Society is unjust. You are still responsible for you.

Reflection 53

Reflect

I won't give up my faith.

Ruminate

No matter who you are or what circumstances you may find yourself in, it's guaranteed that some aspects of your life will seem to limit you. I have seen families give up their faith after the devastation caused by the reckless cruelty of a drunk driver. Good people develop dreaded diseases. Houses burn to the ground, leaving families homeless and distraught. Young men and women are killed on the battlefield, their heartbroken mothers in tears, mourning. Corporate down-sizing, companies closing, people filing for bankruptcy, seeking divorces, pursuing affairs—all these are equal-opportunity "unfairnesses."

We wonder why life seems to become more difficult for some while others seem to escape untouched. But no one is truly untouched. Their devastations may be more private, but take no less a toll. I have encountered millionaires who wrestle to get out of bed in the morning because they are so utterly depressed. Male, female, young, old, black or white—each one of us learns at an early age that life doesn't conform to our wishes. It rarely goes exactly as we might want.

Yet we mustn't abdicate the power to make choices that we do have. And one of those choices is faith.

Remember

My faith "cheat sheet"

- Everything that exists has a source. Creator.
- Disconnection from our Creator, each other, and our planet was not intended. Redeemer.
- Reality is more than material. Spirit.

Reflection 54

Reflect

I will let nothing stop me.

Ruminate

You may not be able to bring back a loved one, but you must not let your grief rob you of loving those who remain in your life.

You may not be able to afford the latest-model SUV, but you must not let that prevent you from getting where you need to go.

You may not have the capital required to begin your new business, but you must not let that keep you from selling your product to friends and neighbors.

You may not be qualified for the new position that just opened up in your company, but you must not let that keep you from enrolling in night courses at a community college.

You may not have the partner you long to love and to help parent your children, but you must not let that keep you from parenting your kids wisely and helping them be parented as much as possible by their other parent.

Remember

I may not now have everything I need to achieve my goals, but I have *me* and I'll get started.

Reflection 55

Reflect

I'm angry.

Ruminate

Go ahead, say it, "It's easy for *you,* Preacher Man, to say, 'Life is not fair.' Look at what you've got! Look at where you are. If you were me, you'd be angry too!"

I truly feel your pain. However, Langston Hughes penned the phrase that expresses my sentiments: "Life for me ain't been no crystal stair." In *Reposition Yourself* I talk about where I come from, my trials, disappointments. I only talk about a tiny percentage of them. There are many more! I have been angry. Angry at how unfair life is. Angry about racism. Angry at God. Angry at myself. What I have not done, however, is succumb to rage and blame. I realize that anger without action leaves me bitter and not better!

If you're angry, be angry. Get it out and move on! Voice your outrage and grief. Say it over and over, write it down and burn it in a bonfire, vent to your best friend, or scream it to your counselor. LIFE ISN'T FAIR. Get it out of your system as much and as regularly as you need to, but do not allow anger to fester in you and halt you in your progress forward.

Remember

Anger resides in the lap of fools. —Ecclesiastes 7:9 (NIV)

Reflection 56

Reflect

My maturity is born of suffering.

Ruminate

"You intended to harm me, but God intended it for good to accomplish what is now being done, the saving of many lives." —Genesis 50:20 (NIV)

Joseph's maturity, born of suffering, serves as a model for us. (See Reflection 41.) Similarly, you must have faith to know that someday you will be able to say the same thing to your enemies, persecutors, those who called you a loser, and those who hurt you along the way. What they intended to harm you, deter you, defeat you, God will use to make you stronger, to help you learn to find inner healing, to secure your success.

What is it that your suffering is moving you toward?

Remember

Suffering can be the basis for the passion that fuels my dream. God has the power to transform even the most horrendous events in my life into catalysts for unimaginable success.

Reflection 57

Reflect

I will persevere.

Ruminate

No matter how sharp the pain of life is, you must dig in deep and never give up. We must not give up on ourselves or one another. No matter how old you are, what you've been through, or how many battles you feel that you've lost, it's never too late to reposition yourself.

Repositioning yourself may require you to rekindle the cold ashes of what was once your fiery passion. You will have to allow yourself to hope again and to take small steps toward the goal of becoming who God created you to be.

Or it may include picking up a new trade or skill. It may mean going back to school.

Either way, it will not be easy. You will need to follow through.

Remember

I must persevere to prevail.

Reflection 58

Reflect

_____ is my personal hero.

Ruminate

Choose your personal hero. One of the best ways we can envision our own success is to have clear role models or personal heroes. Whether it's Lance Armstrong beating cancer to win the Tour de France, Toni Morrison winning the Nobel Prize for literature, or Nelson Mandela overcoming the brutality of racism to become the president of South Africa, you look to individuals who inspire you. Heroes and role models are proof that where we want to go does in fact exist.

Remember

I have exemplary role models among the ordinary people in my life—friends, family members, co-workers, pastors, counselors. I will recognize them as the heroes they are to me.

Reflection 59

Reflect

I am a student of my own success.

Ruminate

Education isn't always confined to the hallowed halls of esteemed learning institutions. We all must get an education even if we have to inhale our learning from secondhand smoke. If you can't go back to school to sharpen your skills, you can read. All universities are not made of stone nor all teachers stationed in front of chalkboards. Life is a school. Books and even magazines are an opportunity to sharpen our minds.

Success comes through exposure. Reading is one of the ways we expose ourselves. In church we say that faith comes by hearing. What that means is that what we are exposed to, what is preached and taught from God's Word, shapes what we believe.

You must nourish your heart, imagination, and mind with the rich fertilizer of words and images from the fields that you would someday like to harvest. Your dreams may be on a starvation diet if you are not reading articles, gathering stats, surfing the net, or in other ways feeding yourself with knowledge to grow your deepest goals and dreams. I should be able to look at your reading habits and see not only what you do but have some glimpse into what you are going to do next.

Remember

I feed my own dreams by continually educating myself.

Reflection 60

Reflect

What's holding me back?

Ruminate

It is important for you to acknowledge those areas of your life where you have suffered injustice and defeat. You might even want to make a list of events, people, and incidents that you believe have held you back and kept you from achieving more. You may want to discuss your list with friends, family members, your pastor, or a qualified counselor. If you need to do this, it can be a healthy part of repositioning yourself. Make the list. Discuss the list. Then throw it away.

You cannot despair over it and become bitter. Do not, for any reason, resign yourself to less than you were created for. Take heart and empower yourself with education, exemplary role models, and the latest information about your desired area of interest.

If you are already bitter, angry, and despairing, those things will hold you back. But, there *is* hope. Those are all emotions. Little by little you can retrain yourself. It is easier said than done, but it *can* be done. And you can do it.

Remember

Despite the unfairness of life, I have freedoms and options for which my ancestors labored and died trying to provide for me. I will let nothing hold me back.

Reflection 61

Reflect

I refuse to accept limitations and defeat.

Ruminate

If you refuse to be handcuffed by the limitations that your environment, upbringing, or peers set for you, then you will discover a limitless source of self-confidence and resilience.

If you refuse to accept defeat when momentary setbacks alter your plans, then you are well on your way to repositioning yourself for your next stage of success.

Remember

I am wise and strong enough to dare to rise above and beyond the limitations of my life and what appear to be past defeats.

Reflection 62

Reflect

I root for the underdog in me.

Ruminate

It's human nature that we're inclined to root for the underdog. We want to see someone weaker, younger, poorer, or less talented win. Our innate sense of fairness wants to level the playing field and for the ill favored to overthrow the stronger, older, richer, or more talented. If David can defeat Goliath, it's possible for us to pick up only our slingshot and face our giants.

We are all underdogs. If we accept what life dictates to us, we are not likely to win. But if we dare to rise above and beyond the limitations of our lives, we have the underdog's chance—the opportunity for an exciting victory.

Remember

Rooting for the underdog in me means repositioning myself to grow stronger and wiser and being more willing to dream and dream big.

Reflection 63

Reflect

I can bounce back.

Ruminate

Today, when someone tells me they hope to "bounce back," my mind goes to those hard plastic Super Balls from long ago. In order to reposition ourselves toward the life without limits that we all crave, we must be like the skyrocketing bounces of those Super Balls that always come back for more, having lost little of their inherent force.

Bouncing back from our mistakes is not just a requirement for repositioning ourselves but a strategy for discovery as well. The process of bouncing back is to examine our mis-

takes and learn from our less-than-best choices and to transform our errors into opportunities. We not only bounce back,
but we come back stronger.

Remember

I embrace the fact that failing is part of life, and I rebound
higher and farther than where I started.

Reflection 64

Reflect

It's OK to be a quitter.

Ruminate

I'm a terrible golfer. I tried to be good golfer but I was awful. And you know what? It didn't bother me. I could laugh at myself. I value the new terms I learned that enable me to converse with friends for whom golf is a passion. I enjoyed some exercise in some of the most beautiful settings around the country. And I discovered that I was not cut out to be a golfer! It's just not my thang, and that's OK.

The temptation for many of us when we don't succeed at something we undertake is either to continue to torture ourselves (refuse to quit) or to end the new venture, feeling like a quitter. It's been said that "quitters never prosper." I disagree.

Quitters do prosper if they know that they do not have passion for a given activity and if they learn from it what they can—about themselves, about others who do enjoy it, about life—and move on to discover their true passions.

After my flirtation with golf, I discovered that I much prefer lifting weights in order to stay fit. It's an activity that I can enjoy over the long haul and patiently progress in.

Remember

To quit is to create a place for what fits.

Reflection 65

Reflect

I will push out into "deep water."

Ruminate

"Push out into deep water and let your nets out for a catch."

—JESUS

Simon said, "Master, we've been fishing hard all night and haven't caught even a minnow. But if you say so, I'll let out the nets." It was no sooner said than done—a huge haul of fish, straining the nets past capacity. They waved to their partners in the other boat to come help them. They filled both boats, nearly swamping them with the catch.

—LUKE 5:4-7 (THE MESSAGE)

The biblical passage above is striking to me for several reasons. It's interesting that Jesus tells Peter to "push out into deep water" as if perhaps he has been casting in the shallows. Sometimes it's easy for us to stay in the safety of shallow water, splashing and casting, wading and wandering around, without ever risking deeper water. We stay in our current position rather than asking for a promotion or applying elsewhere. We resign ourselves to our present relationship even after it's clear to both parties that it's going nowhere.

Shallow water feels so much safer. We can both see and touch the bottom. But this apparent security also imposes limitations. Just as in Simon Peter's case, we have to learn that the deeper water holds the fish!

Remember

Living my life without limits requires that I take confident risks.

Reflection 66

Reflect

I keep my mind open.

Ruminate

So often we plateau on a level of competent complacency where nothing we do seems to break us through to the next level. We see promotions given to individuals who have been with the company a shorter time than we have. We see our attempts to start our own business sputter and die as investors change their minds, market trends change, and opportunities for retail space pass us by.

But it can all change when someone points out a subtle way we can adjust our approach. Like a tennis pro adjusting the angle of her racket as she serves, or a golf player altering his stance and the angle of his hips, we often discover that the best advice can come from unexpected places.

Keep an open mind to suggestions, even criticism, that come from people you least expect. Even people you don't like, you know don't like you, you don't feel have the slightest knowledge of your areas of concern—anyone can shed useful light on your situation. An outsider often brings a fresh perspective that can innovate tired systems and worn-out procedures. I encourage you to seek out the perspective of others, particularly if you are struggling on your journey toward your goals. The insight of those ahead of you is invaluable, and I cannot emphasize the significance of a generous mentor. However, you must also be on the lookout for the unexpected and unorthodox perspectives of those whom you wouldn't normally be inclined to consider. The result may astound you.

Remember

I listen with an open mind to unexpected feedback.

Reflection 67

Reflect

I choose wisely.

Ruminate

If you are to reposition yourself for success, my friend, you must give yourself permission to close doors behind you, to lay down some of the balls that you're juggling when you pick up a new one, and to say no to good opportunities if they're not advancing you strategically toward the large goals you've established for yourself.

I'm often surprised at the gifted, intelligent, driven individuals who, when they come to me for advice—torn between two job offers, career moves, or appealing opportunities—haven't already attended to the ABCs of who they are and what they're about. They haven't determined what their brand is. (See Reflection 9 and *Reposition Yourself,* pp. 87–90, for discussion of "branding yourself.")

Remember

Too many positive options can be a limitation. Spending too much time deciding among various options can indicate I have not clarified my goals.

Reflection 68

Reflect

I know my "power lures."

Ruminate

Identify three key attributes that you offer in any meeting with colleagues and friends or three virtues that you bring to a relationship or social encounter. I like to call these "deliverables," or, to use a fishing term, "power lures." Deliverables are not aspects of our personality that we have to contrive or work at producing. No, they are natural characteristics.

I went fishing with a friend and discovered "super bait"—an artificial bait in bright neon yellow and pink colors, with a strong "natural" smell. It reminded me of caviar made out of Play-Doh. Wow, did it attract fish. It got the job done!

Your power lures are your fine internal qualities (physical

qualities don't count here!) that draw people to you. Know what they are and use them.

Remember

My strong, positive natural qualities reveal me to me, they authenticate me, they indicate who I really am.

Reflection 69

Reflect

I will be either hot or cold—not lukewarm.

Ruminate

I know your deeds, that you are neither cold nor hot. I wish you were either one or the other! So, because you are lukewarm—neither hot nor cold—I am about to spit you out of my mouth.

—Revelation 3:15–16 (NIV)

One of the greatest obstacles to success is mediocrity. The small, quiet enemy is stealing moments from our day, sabotaging opportunities to our advancement, and transforming our strengths into weaknesses. Mediocrity results from accepting the second-rate, the average (or below average), that which is middling, ordinary, commonplace, run of the mill, and middle of the road. Rather than striving for excellence, for the extraordinary, the best, the remarkable, and first-rate, mediocrity begs you to stay put and resign yourself to the status quo.

Mediocrity is your own voice in your ear, saying, "You silly woman, you really think he could be interested in you?" Or: "You old fool, there's no way you can go back to school and earn that degree." Or: "Your own business? You can't even balance your checkbook!" Mediocrity places on you the blinders of the mundane—the bills, the kids, the laundry, the stress, the illness, the breakup—so that you cannot see beyond the present moment.

Defend, overcome, achieve are the ways we overcome the elements of mediocrity, such as debt, liabilities, and limited resources, that prevent us from having success.

Remember

Armed with some new insights and the unlimited resources available through God's strength, I am empowered to excel.

Reflection 70

Reflect

I will reposition first. Announce later.

Ruminate

We don't always know what is around the corner.

If I had known that I would be leaving West Virginia to start a new life in Dallas, Texas, I would never have bought a brand-new house in my home state, and I would have avoided the expense of maintaining two house payments in two different states for a year, hoping that the old house would sell before I ran out of money and lost my new one!

Reposition yourself *before* you announce what you think is going to happen next.

Remember

As I reposition myself, my actions may require no announcements.

Reflection 71

Reflect

I am becoming a make-it-happen person.

Ruminate

Accept no decree—whether from God or government or anyone—about how you should live your life, without being an active participant. It's up to you. (God has given you choice.) Stop waiting for others to lead you to where only you can go yourself. Stop blaming the past. It's easy to embrace the role of victim, of loser, of the one who's not smart enough, not good enough, not educated enough, not financially sound enough. When you accept such limitations for yourself, you don't have to worry about being disappointed. It doesn't hurt to fall if you're already on the floor!

Be what I call a make-it-happen person. These are the

people who see what is coming and they make it happen rather than hope it happens or react to what happens. These people know where power is located. Some teach that it is in heaven. Some teach that it is in the White House. But the Bible teaches that it is in you: "Now unto him that is able to do exceeding abundantly above all that we ask or think, according to the power that *worketh in us* . . ." —Ephesians 3:20 (KJV)

Remember

The power is in *me*.

Reflection 72

Reflect

I align with the challenges of change in my life.

Ruminate

The only certain thing about life is change. Stopping change is futile. But planning for change is not. To reposition yourself, anticipate change.

We're forced to keep the change in our lives whether we want to or not. Realize that the best of situations can turn on a dime and become the worst crisis we've faced. So many of life's hardships derive their power from the unexpected timing of the punch that catches us off guard. We all struggle, day in and day out.

No matter how faith-filled, how financially responsible, how politically correct you are, or how congenial you may be with others, you will inevitably find yourself from time to time facing moments that threaten you like a terrorist attack.

However, some people manage the challenges better than others and are thereby able to expend their energies on winning rather than merely enduring the undetected Scud missiles that come out of nowhere, threatening to detonate their careful plans with the shrapnel of the unexpected.

The good news, however, is that we can convert the storms of opposition into the wind beneath our wings.

Remember

I can use experiences that require change—even ones in which I'm pushed to the wall—to break through barriers and expand my limits.

Reflection 73

Reflect

I reposition myself in stages.

Ruminate

Sons are a heritage from the Lord, children a reward from him. Like arrows in the hands of a warrior are sons born in one's youth. Blessed is the man whose quiver is full of them. They will not be put to shame when they contend with their enemies in the gate.

—PSALM 127:3-5 (NIV)

The powerful analogy of the psalmist compares the potential of children to the power of arrows. The quiver is the place where arrows wait to be used. It is the place of possibility. It is the place where patience comes into play. Potentials are yet to be galvanized into action.

There are three stages of parenting revealed in this text. One is the state of reservation; the second is the state of retraction; the third is the state of release.

The overarching idea is not about children as much as it is about positioning to harvest the fruit of your labors. You may be an adult and still need to go through these three stages—reservation, retraction, release—to hit the target in your life, whether it involves business, marriage, or whatever your goal is.

If you feel you have not been positioned correctly, I have good news. It is not too late to go back through the process of reservation (taking the time to meditate on the new goals and ideas, associate with people who do what you want to do), retraction (go into hibernation and get the skills you need for the dream you have), and then release (go for the dreams that have eluded you before). Repositioning is about having a second chance to realign what wasn't properly directed the first time.

Remember

The stages of repositioning—reservation, retraction, release.

Reflection 74

Reflect

My repositioning begins with reservation.

Ruminate

We live in a world where three-year-olds have tattoos and five-year-old girls are wearing heels and makeup. Giving children things prematurely is not a blessing. Some things are reserved until you grow up and grow into them. Sexual relationships are reserved for adults and not meant for children. Many good things are not good if they are granted prematurely.

Sometimes we adults get things prematurely, before we grow into them. Your life becomes bigger, and success crushes you.

Understand that delayed does not mean denied (see Reflection 18), and that just because you have to wait for it doesn't mean that it isn't coming. The first word they shout on the firing range is "ready." Are you ready for what is about to happen? Is your home ready? Do you have a system in place for winning? Often there are systems in place for losing, but little is done to prepare you for winning. Have you ever thought about what achieving your dream would do to your life? Do you have the systems ready to accommodate that level of busy? Are you prepared for what the demands will be when you are there?

Remember

I am preparing for the fallout of my success.

Reflection 75

Reflect

My repositioning continues with retraction.

Ruminate

It's part of the process to experience what some have called taking one step forward and two steps backward. That's retraction. Like an arrow in a bow, most people go backward before they shoot forward.

What do you do when you can see the goal but you keep losing ground? How do you manage the frustration of having it in your sights and yet seeing circumstances thwart the aspirations you hope to realize?

You understand that it is normal to retract before release. You roll with the back flow and keep your eye on the target, and keep preparing to shoot forward.

So draw back your bow. Accept those steps backward, those thing that seem to thwart your progress. Keep your eye on your goal, intensify your focus.

The aiming stage is the retracting stage. It is when the arrow is retracted that it is also aimed. It takes strength and discipline not to release the arrow too soon. You must be patient and maintain the retraction until the time is right and your release can be as strategic as possible. You want to retract until you know the tension in the bow supports the launch so that the arrow reaches the target and penetrates the bull's-eye.

I am sure that my aim has been improved by my agony. You will shoot farther because of the retraction.

Remember

Setbacks are really set*ups* for success.

Reflection 76

Reflect

My repositioning culminates with release.

Ruminate

If you take a common garden hose and temporarily restrict the flow of water by bending it, the force of the water will be all the greater when you straighten it out. In a similar way, those of us who have experienced setbacks in life often release and shoot farther precisely because of the setback.

Anticipate your moment of release. Vindicate your pain and retraction with the power of your release. With the force of a pent-up need comes the jubilation of freedom. You can never know how free you are until you understand how bound and pent up you once were.

Release is celebration, fulfillment.

All of us who enjoy health do not understand how glorious it is until we have seen someone who lost it and gets it back again. This is the power of release.

Celebration is as intoxicating as the wedding night of a virgin man who through abstinence has now come to the consummation with the freedom of full expression.

Fulfillment is that feeling of the student who struggled all through school, laboring to write papers and take tests, and who now graduates.

It is the energy of that first generation of my people who voted and women now achieving their dreams in a country where they were once considered property.

Remember

I anticipate the joy of success as I reposition myself.

Reflection 77

Reflect

I manage my blessings wisely.

Ruminate

The way many authors write about prosperity is much like parents who spoil a child. It may sound good and sweet, when you're getting blessed, but eventually the result is a spoiled brat who whines for things but doesn't have the sense to sustain what has been given.

Learning how to manage and disentangle yourself from the financial limitations that clutter your life can be one of the most liberating feelings you'll ever experience. You will not likely become rich, but you need never *worry* about money again. You will feel in control because there's not a crisis, secure because there's a strategy, and fulfilled because you're finally facing the facts.

Remember

I am responsible for attaining and managing what God provides.

Reflection 78

Reflect

I receive the power that comes with persecution.

Ruminate

The water hoses of the sixties and atrocities like the bombing of a church that killed four little girls shamed the nation into changing its racist Jim Crow policy and ushered in the civil rights amendments. Who can ignore the power of persecution? Certainly not Christians! We know salvation was procured only after crucifixion. It was not what Jesus said on the cross that redeemed us; it was what our Redeemer *suffered* on the cross.

Receive the blessings from your afflictions. I am positive that had I not suffered my little afflictions, I would not be so focused today, for my focus comes from my struggle. I call my afflictions light ones and am embarrassed to include them on a page that speaks of the stench of four burning girls who perished in a Sunday school classroom.

Are your persecutions truly severe? Only you know. What I know is that if you're reading this page, you have not suffered unto death, that you can reposition yourself and live your life with the power that comes with persecution. This is the reward of those who have been pulled to the breaking point.

Remember

Anguish precedes victory.

Reflection 79

Reflect

My options—the choices I have—determine my quality of life.

Ruminate

Life is easier and more comfortable if you have financial resources, but the quality of our life is not conditioned upon this fact. We are not without choices or resources even if we don't have as much money as we'd like.

List the options available to you now and tailor a plan to fit what is best given those options you have. If you start looking with a positive attitude, you will find that there are a lot of ways to get back home from the Land of Oz. Clicking your heels may only be one way, Dorothy.

Then reposition yourself for more options.

Remember

I always have choices. I have to "see" them.

Reflection 80

Reflect

I am anchored in the moment.

Ruminate

You must always be grateful for where you are right now, if you are to remain anchored in the present moment and not regretting the past or living conditionally for the future.

I have learned the secret of being content in any and every situation, whether well fed or hungry, whether living in plenty or in want. I can do everything through him who gives me strength.

—PHILIPPIANS 4:12–13 (NIV)

I am not saying this because I am in need, for I have learned to be content whatever the circumstances. I know what it is to be in need, and I know what it is to have plenty.

—PHILIPPIANS 4:11–12 (NIV)

I personally have been privileged to sleep in the penthouse suite of some of the world's most opulent five-star hotels. I have also slept in the back of the church and at Grandma's house on a cot on the back porch. I believe I am able to appreciate what I have because I realize that my level of contentment is not dependent on my surroundings.

Remember

I maintain a panoramic view of my good and bad experiences.

Reflection 81

Reflect

While I reposition myself to provide the best I can for my children, I make sure they learn what struggle teaches.

Ruminate

Greatness often comes through struggle. Most members of a first generation—first to be educated, first to own businesses, first to have wealth—have a challenging time getting their children to embrace their values. The children hear us but don't fully appreciate the message we're sending them, because they haven't had our experiences. They have not learned firsthand the lessons that poverty and struggle can teach.

One successful man said to his wife, "We gave our children everything except what made us great."

"What's that?" she asked.

He sighed and replied, "Struggle!"

While struggle is not the *only* way greatness is born, it is hard for the privileged and pampered to have the experiences and challenges that build character and virtue.

Remember

As I reposition myself for living without limits, I must be sure I set boundaries for my children, and other young people I influence, that will allow them to become the great ones of their generation.

Reflection 82

Reflect

I appreciate my priceless blessings.

Ruminate

. . . a family that loves me.

. . . knowing I worked my way to the top.

. . . hearing a child laugh.

. . . the calming sway of the mighty ocean.

. . . a friend who couldn't go to bed after the party until I got home safely.

. . . a child with two front teeth missing singing a solo completely out of tune, smiling BIG!

Remember

I include such free and priceless items in my personal portfolio of blessings. I keep my own list of priceless blessings in mind, always.

Reflection 83

Reflect

I will face my financial fears.

Ruminate

If you don't have a financial plan and lack an awareness of where you are financially, it's impossible to reposition yourself. If you hit a wall of fear, shame, and guilt every time your spending habits come up, it's time to face the challenge. Get help if you need to.

Face yourself and the emotional baggage you have regarding money. Look it squarely in the eye. Journal and discuss it with someone who's ahead of you in this area—a friend, a family member, someone from church. Be honest with yourself and be honest with them. Don't lie or put a spin on past mistakes. If you wasted money on clubbing and eating out, acknowledge it. Plan how you will prevent your-self from repeating the pattern.

David possessed the strength and confidence to square off against a terrifying foe because he had defeated the smaller threats along the way. (Read in the Bible, I Samuel 17 and pay particular attention to verses 34–36.) He viewed those past encounters with lions and bears as God's training ground for facing and defeating Goliath. The future king learned to fight for his flock, sheep by sheep, and from that battle he learned how to go into a situation that others viewed as insurmountable.

This is how we must learn to reposition ourselves as we examine our financial lives and the role money plays in who we are and what we do. One bill at a time. One debt at a time. One savings deposit at a time. One budget cycle at a time.

Remember

Financial well-being is only one aspect of what it means to thrive. Financial peace begins with willingness to look hon-estly at my spending and handling of money.

Reflection 84

Reflect

I will trust a financial accountability partner.

Ruminate

Repositioning your finances involves finding someone you can turn to when the urge to splurge hits full force. Just as a recovering addict has a sponsor, someone who has been sober and successfully in recovery for a long period, you need someone who can ask the hard questions and provide some strong feedback.

Do not choose someone who will add to your natural guilt, shame, fear, and insecurity. Instead find an encourager, a person who knows what it means to struggle with your issues and is farther down the road than you. Perhaps you can even set up a regular time together to discuss and assess your progress. This person works the way a personal accountant works for wealthy people—keeps you on task. However, this person is no substitute for you to intervene on your own behalf and set a course that will allow you to prosper on all levels.

Remember

Openly sharing my financial status, goals, mistakes, and fears with someone I trust, who will hold me accountable, is part of my financial growth.

Reflection 85

Reflect

I reposition with an attitude of gratitude, and aptitude.

Ruminate

Beginning with a check for eight dollars that I received as a boy from Mrs. Minerva Coles, a neighbor back in West Virginia, for mowing—or should I say scalping—her yard, I have learned how to value hard work and appreciate a dollar earned. I have delivered newspapers, sold fresh fish from the back of my father's red pickup truck, dug ditches, and worked the night shift at a Union Carbide plant. Through these difficult, yet transforming jobs, God taught me much about attitude, gratitude, and aptitude. I learned that I didn't want to spend my life lifting a shovel to dig a trench. I learned what it meant to use present labor as a means to future fulfillment.

Discipline, budgeting, timing, and cost efficiency—I received these lessons not in an MBA program or a Fortune 500 company, but in the sweat, blisters, and bloodshed of my first twenty-five years of living.

God has allowed me to take those humble skills and follow my creative passions—music, drama, film, books—transforming those passions into lucrative businesses.

Remember

As I reposition myself, I maintain an attitude of gratitude toward God and those who have helped me, and I constantly develop new aptitudes.

Reflection 86

Reflect

I accept life's inevitable losses.

Ruminate

Every winner expects to lose along the way.

One of the problems I have with the way faith is taught today is that we do not prepare people for the fact that faith may not get them what they want, even if they do pray. This name-it-claim-it idea is dangerous propaganda. It makes people think that success is an Easy-Bake recipe—do this, do that, tell God how you'd like it. I get concerned when I hear people teaching that faith in God ensures success or that a certain offering given to the church will guarantee a blessing.

It takes a combination of faith and works, success and struggles, failures and fortitude, to produce success.

A sales trainer said something I will never forget: "I do not have to teach you how to win. All I have to teach you is how to face rejection and not give up on winning." Sales reps who win big are not ones who are never denied; they just do not allow the "no" of one customer to become a prognosis of fatality. Great salesmen do not allow a "no" to define them. They know that losing is a part of winning.

Like a child who stumbles his way into walking, most great people learn what not to do by failing along their way up.

Remember

I learn much about winning by losing.

Reflection 87

Reflect

I value my losses.

Ruminate

What I do with my losses:

- Minimize the damage of my losses wherever I can.
- Get some distance from the loss, whether in perspective, time, or both; then reassess what transpired.
- List mistakes that contributed to the loss, and note how many of them are in my control.
- Make a strategy of how I can avoid those mistakes next time.
- Note mistakes that were beyond my control, and chalk them up to the cost of living on the planet.

- Blame no one. Hold no grudges.
- Forgive myself and others. Harbor no guilt.
- Remind myself that delays are not denials.

Remember

I make my losses count for something, by winning next time.

Reflection 88

Reflect

I learn to embrace success, with its challenges.

Ruminate

Our success can create a new set of complications, in our own minds and emotions and spirits, and in our relationships. Fulfilling our potential often creates a complex set of challenges with those around us. We'll likely have to learn to peel away labels that others will begin to stick on us as we ascend to new heights. They can reduce the complexity and uniqueness of our hard work and accomplishments to a handful of clichés, adjectives, and labels.

Can this be avoided? Not in my experience or from what I've observed and discussed with other successful individuals from diverse backgrounds. Can it be minimized and managed so that it will not impede your ascent and damage your relationships? Absolutely yes!

We have to *learn* to enjoy our success to the fullest. You think it comes naturally, effortlessly, but it doesn't always. Success brings its own set of internal and relational challenges. Mastering them is another way we grow and further develop character.

Remember

I greet success not as a solution to all my challenges, but as an interesting new set of challenges.

Reflection 89

Reflect

The past is past.

Ruminate

Once we rebound from mistakes and reposition our lives into power, we will still be reminded of the past. Despite seeing God, time after time, create ministry out of misery, I still encounter successful people carrying enormous loads of guilt, shame, anger, fear, and anxiety. Their pasts continue to haunt their present and to inhibit their future. Many, no matter how successful their careers and families, view themselves as victims and failures rather than as strivers and survivors. As if it were not enough to have to found the strength to thrive in an often unforgiving world, they have the added burden of surviving their own remorse, shame, and guilt.

Once they release the burdens of the past, they continue their journey with a lighter load. They have to grasp what Jesus meant: "My yoke is easy and my burden is light." —Matthew 11:30 (NIV)

Remember

What I've done or haven't done; who's hurt me or who I've hurt; who I've been with; who I've walked out on or who's walked out on me—all is past. I can reposition myself *now*!

Reflection 90

Reflect

I step into my destiny, for my generation.

Ruminate

You are armed with the tools you need to succeed. You are clear on your seasons, convinced of your contribution, aware of your own frailties, and flexible enough to adapt to unexpected setbacks. You are ready to live in a generation where for women, the glass ceiling has been turned into a glass slipper and for those of African descent and others of color, the playing field has never been more level. You have no limitations. This is a new day with new opportunities.

No, things are not perfect. Yes, the world remains grossly unfair. You will have to rest sometimes, pray sometimes, forgive sometimes, and, yes, even fight sometimes. But this is also true: if you have the courage to believe, nothing shall be impossible.

Remember

I let go of the limitations placed on previous generations and I step confidently into today's possibilities.

Reflection 91

Reflect

I've got influence.

Ruminate

Influence is fuel for your power base. It's very difficult to have it and not use it. Good stewardship of success is managing your influence without it becoming contaminated by those who seek to use you.

Influence is always monitored by those around you. If you use it well, and others see it, they will try to harness it and use it. For example, if you have influence or "pull" with the boss, someone will try to deliver their message through your mouth. The most difficult part of influence isn't getting it, but maintaining influence.

Protect your sphere of influence. Some will position themselves around you just to gain influence. What can you do when you have built a name with integrity but others with less integrity hitch up to you like a trailer on the back of a truck and go along for the ride? Unfortunately, sometimes there's not much you can do! Be aware of who is using your name and message to send their agenda. Your name and reputation quickly become diluted and your message corrupted when others usurp your identity.

Be careful about the company you keep. You inadvertently give a certain amount of power to people just by being seen with them. Often you are held guilty by association. If I'm seen with a member of either political party, suddenly it's assumed by the public that I support that party's entire agenda! This way of making assumptions is almost universal, no matter how famous or obscure we are. Choose carefully those with whom you associate.

Watch out for hitchhikers! Some people siphon off your energy, attention, and influence. They do not earnestly want a relationship with you, but they need to borrow your influence or they want to go along for the ride. But that is not the worst part. The worst part is the baggage that they bring along. And you often inherit their enemies simply by your silence.

Remember

I choose the people in my life.

Reflection 92

Reflect

I know my twins.

Ruminate

Reconcile who you are publicly with who you are privately. We all have a set of twins inside of us, but they are not identical. These twins are extremely different yet share the same space just as fraternal twins do.

One of them is our ideal self, the person we want to be and we want all who know us to believe that we are. But then there is the real self, who may be less polished, may be limited, and may lack the skills to navigate an effective relationship. The real person has blemishes that we try fiercely to keep from view.

These two "selves" often wrestle for control, fighting—no, warring—one against the other until we are miserable. The attempt to live up to our ideal selves depletes us and causes discontentment with our real selves. This dissonance is the inner turmoil we struggle with, usually at home. (Those who want to love us tire of the constant battle waging inside us. This takes domestic disputes to a whole new level!)

The solution is this: whatever we feed is what we grow. If we feed the real person and home life, it will grow stronger. If we feed the work life and the ideal self, it will grow stronger. You need both, and we have to channel our attention and effort, in a balanced way, into both.

Budget your emotional resources. Most of us lack the balance that it takes to be naturally effective in both our business and private lives. It takes effort. Know your twins and feed them as equally as you can.

Remember

There is nothing more beneficial to me and to those around me than to be a person who is balanced and not moving to extremes.

Reflection 93

Reflect

God knows my twins.

Ruminate

God helps you balance the ideal you and the real you. God provides balance in your turbocharged life, counsels you, shows you how to realign what you accomplish at work with who you are at home. God gives you a life that is defined by more than what you have achieved—people who wait for you and see you as more than what you do, who value you for who you are.

God shows you how to take your success home with you. As you reposition yourself for a life without limits, reposition your priorities so that pursuit of success in your home is at the top. Remind the people in your life why you're doing what you do outside of the house by sharing your heart, your time, and your concerns with them. Let them in and keep them with you.

Remember

I depend on God's grace and direction to maintain the pace and passion of my success.

Reflection 94

Reflect

I never forget where I came from.

Ruminate

Most successful people do not intend to lose touch with the place from which they came. Some do suddenly think they're better than others because they moved out of the hood, got an education, and have a better job. But most successful people just get too busy to keep the old connections. They have less and less in common with old friends, and the family reunion seems to fall at the wrong time in the business cycle. The heritage that once nurtured and inspired them seems like ancient history. Those they associate with nowadays don't share that heritage.

These are reasons, but not excuses.

We must tap into our roots continually, and seek to live out our heritage every day, enjoying the present moment as a precious legacy with which we have been entrusted through the sacrifices of our ancestors. Maybe we find ways to show our families glimpses of the world we now live in so that they can better understand who we are and where we're headed. Perhaps we get honest with ourselves and realize that no matter how much our circumstances and resumes may have changed, there are aspects of us that remain the same, that we are still more like those we grew up with than those we associate with nowadays.

Maintain family traditions from your childhood. It may be inconvenient to attend Sunday dinner at Grandma's once a month, but you will cherish the time with her and other relatives once you're there. If you can afford to travel and visit family for important holidays and birthdays, do it. Find a balance between where you're going and where you've been.

Be honest with yourself. If it's painful to visit your parents because of what happened in the past, then be honest with yourself and them. Perhaps you need to take a sabbatical from family holidays for a few years while you get counseling and deal with your issues. Maybe you need to have a heart-to-heart conversation with a parent or relative who has hurt you. But don't allow yourself to continue returning only to relive the incident; arguing, yelling, and crying will likely only keep your wound open.

Make family time sacred. Whether you're married or single, your life will be enriched if you find a consistent time to connect and really be present with your family.

Remember

I find fulfilling ways to consistently reconnect with those I love and do more than go through the motions with them.

Reflection 95

Reflect

I create new traditions.

Ruminate

Whether with your immediate family or with your family of close friends, celebrate life in fresh, creative ways that contain no baggage from the past. Maybe it's how you celebrate birthdays with your girlfriends or how you and your children recognize the Sabbath as a day of rest. Maybe you've always wanted to have a series of Kwanzaa feasts or go dancing on Valentine's Day.

Repositioning yourself means no limits on the ways you

build family and community. Find some ways to tailor such special occasions to your style and personality.

Remember

Repositioning myself is my opportunity to find new ways to celebrate what is important to me about my family and friends.

Reflection 96

Reflect

I honor those who helped me succeed.

Ruminate

Repeat those special words your grandmother often shared with you. Recite the prayer your father used to pray before dinner each night. Or perhaps have a calligrapher print those meaningful words on beautiful paper for framing. Bring out the mementos of special events when your family really supported you or encouraged your dream. Look at them, relive the moments. Cherish the memories.

Now find ways, limitless ways, to show them honor and gratitude.

Find a way to share stories of your family's past with the

next generation—your own children, nieces and nephews, or young ones you are mentoring.

Remember

I didn't get where I am by myself. Someone helped me get here and I celebrate them.

Reflection 97

Reflect

I share my success.

Ruminate

Many successful individuals go to the opposite extreme of haughtiness. Instead of feeling superior to their families, they remain humble and modestly resist sharing their successes. They may fear being ostracized and misunderstood by those who do not have a context for appreciating the new account they've won or the grad school acceptance letter they've just received.

All families have a backside. Do not allow the pain of the past, the contradictions of the present, or the exposure you've had to "nicely packaged people" in your new life to alienate you from the "not so nice" side of your natural family, spiritual family, or cultural family. They might not be as appealing as the upper echelon of society you now rub elbows with, but they are part of your story.

Most families, however, want to celebrate with you and will appreciate the opportunity to be close to you. Your spirit of humility can still prevail even as you call Aunt Gladys and tell her about your promotion. The entire family feels uplifted by your success!

Do not allow success to cause you to trade in the lifelong legacy of authentic, albeit imperfect relationships, for the simulated, factory-produced, digitally enhanced relationships that have everything—except authenticity and love.

Remember

My success is my entire family's success.

Reflection 98

Reflect

In unity, I find community.

Ruminate

The greatest challenge is to find reasons to unite with others. Pursuing a life of balanced prosperity means giving something back. You have been given to so that you can give to others. Don't apologize for what you have been given and have accomplished with your gifting, just always remember to give back.

Giving may imbue you with a warm, gratifying feeling, but it can quickly turn into heartburn when you realize that there is no end to the line of people in need and that some will quickly attack you when you run out. As CeCe Winans sings so beautifully, "No one knows the cost of the oil in my alabaster box!" It costs you so much more than finances to be a giver. To reposition yourself for ongoing and sustained success, be a generous and compassionate spirit, at the same time realizing that the needs of this world are insatiable.

Remember

The Lord blesses me so I can bless others.

Reflection 99

Reflect

Repositioning necessarily involves *choosing* how I respond to change.

Ruminate

Sometimes we are blindsided by challenges, but sometimes unexpected changes are exactly what we have been praying for—joyful, exciting, blessed. Yet these wished-for changes can require tremendous adjustment. Sometimes more so than unwelcome changes.

One woman who in her mid-thirties married a wonderful man and truly enjoyed her marriage said, "He satisfies needs I didn't even know I had! I'm overwhelmed. I don't know how to deal with it. I'm having to expand on the inside in ways I never expected. I can't explain it—it's wonderful but still not easy."

Another woman about the same age, who had longed to marry and finally had, said something similar: "I'm deliriously happy with him, but surprised at how difficult it is for me to be married. I'm used to doing everything myself. I'm amazed at how capable he is, how much he knows, how able he is to just take charge, but I usually find out his strengths *after* I've started to do things myself. I constantly have to remind myself to back off, thinking, 'Girl, you don't have to do this anymore. He really knows how to do this and better than you!' I'm finding that happiness is really, really hard."

Remember

It's how I *respond* to change that determines the impact change has on my life.

Reflection 100

Reflect

I thrive.

Ruminate

Remain vigilant as you move forward, learning from your past mistakes and forgiving yourself for yesterday's failures.

Look beyond your current definitions of success and ensure that your life is balanced with blessings beyond career, work, and finances. No matter where you are, it's not too late to start over, to begin anew, or grow to a higher level. You have everything you need to reposition yourself, to throw off the limitations of others, and to thrive. You are destined for greatness. Go forward, my brothers and sisters, and get started—your life without limits awaits!

Remember

I remain true to myself and my heart's dreams, never settling for less than my full potential.

List of Topics